MW00795426

SOUL CARE

BECOMING WHOLE
IN A BROKEN WORLD

Mark Finley and Steven Mosley

Pacific Press® Publishing Association
Nampa, Idaho
Oshawa, Ontario, Canada

Edited by Kenneth R. Wade
Designed by Tim Larson
Cover art by Nathan Greene
Cover designed by Palimor Studios

Copyright © 1998 by
Pacific Press® Publishing Association
Printed in the United States of America

ISBN 0-8163-1659-7

01 02 03 04 05 • 7 6 5 4 3

Contents

Finding a Good Shepherd

Most of us know how to take care of our prized possessions pretty well. We like to keep that shiny new sedan tuned up and running smoothly. We like to keep our pets healthy and well groomed. We like to keep our flowerbeds well watered and fertilized.

But there's one possession, one possession of infinite value, that many of us don't nourish very well. We don't seem to be that good at the care and feeding—of the soul.

And too often, the religious things we do on behalf of our souls leave us as empty as ever.

It's as if people today are scrambling to make up for lost time. They've been so busy trying to build a career or trying to hang on to job security. They've been busy getting into a house and raising a family and creating a safe community. They've worked hard. And that's commendable. They've invested so much in building a good life.

But all too often something's missing. Suddenly, they realize the center is falling apart. There's nothing there in the heart. They haven't invested very much in the life of the soul. Their spiritual life has withered away.

Could this account for why they have so much stress at work? Maybe that's why so many marriages are breaking up. Maybe that's why so many communities are unsafe. We've neglected spiritual values.

And so people are scrambling to make up for lost time. They want to put something in that center part of their lives. Thomas Moore's book *Care of the Soul* recently became a huge best-seller. Suddenly people wanted to know about the inner life.

Someone else came up with, *Chicken Soup for the Soul*. Others put together a *Handbook for the Soul*. Still others outlined ways to get in touch with our spirituality or mapped out ways to find our "soul mate."

Today, it almost seems, as one book reviewer put it, that any book with the word "soul" or "spirituality" in its title is guaranteed to land on the New York Times bestseller list.

We're rediscovering our souls. We're coming to grips with the fact that a world crammed with dazzling video games, a world full of pay-per-view drama, a world overflowing with Internet info—can still be a pretty empty place.

We need to rediscover the center. We need to rediscover that vital center that holds everything else together.

And this is the center; this is it—a personal relationship with God. That's what the nurture of the human soul is all about. It's not just about religion. It's not just about doing certain things. It's about developing a real relationship with the One who made us, the One who created our hearts and minds. That's at the foundation of how we develop wholeness in our souls.

Psalm 23 paints a beautiful picture of that kind of wholeness. David, the young shepherd, had discovered that God could be his Shepherd. He could be a faithful companion. David invested time in that relationship.

And this is how he describes the result recorded in Psalm 23:

"He makes me to lie down in green pastures; He leads me beside the still waters. He restores my soul; He leads me in the paths of righteousness for His name's sake" (Psalm 23:2, 3, NKJV).

David had found the center. His soul was being nourished. He was at peace, like a lamb feeding in green pastures beside still, clear waters. He was led down the right path.

David had a Good Shepherd.

Finding a Shepherd

How do we develop that kind of relationship with God? That's the question. How do we get to the point where we are nurtured by God—in green pastures, beside still waters?

We want to invest in the kind of Soul Care that will really give our lives a center that will hold everything together. We want to see positive changes. We want to be changed from the inside out.

A recent Gallup poll of people's religious beliefs and practices uncovered some interesting facts. These are statistics taken from the American public, but I believe they reflect what is happening all over the Western world. More than nine out of ten people polled still believe God exists, and what's more, 95 percent say that religious experience is still important for them.

BUT, nine out of ten don't open the Bible—even once a week. Forty-two per cent of the American public actually believes the Bible is the infallible Word of God. And yet only 10 per cent read it regularly.

When the poll examined Protestants, in particular, the figures weren't much better. Almost half could say that yes, the Bible is God's Word. But only 16 per cent read it on a daily basis.

Clearly there's a gap between our beliefs and our practices. Most of us say we recognize God's voice in Scripture, but we're not too good at listening to it.

We need to recover a sense of discovery in God's Word. We need to learn how to listen again. Without that, God has no way of touching our lives and nurturing our souls.

The Gallup poll I mentioned earlier examined individuals in many different ways. They were divided according to age, church affiliation, giving patterns, educational background, etc.

But only one grouping stood out as truly distinctive—those who read the Bible regularly. They measured the highest in matters of belief and moral behavior. Frequent Bible readers were consistently more involved in helping others and putting their faith into practice.

Out of all the statistics gathered by the poll, this one thing came through clearly—listening to the

Word made a difference. All the other "religious" things the poll examined were secondary.

In this chapter, I'd like to zero in on the "how to." I'd like to get as practical as possible. How do we build a healthy spiritual life on a daily basis? What are the specific steps we can take from here to there?

I'm going to share what has helped me enormously. This is the bottom line, folks. Here's how our souls are nurtured day by day.

Learning to listen

It all begins with listening to God's Word. We've got to recover the skill of listening. It's essential for spiritual growth that we hear again God's voice in our lives.

The prophet Isaiah gives us a beautiful picture of this: "The sovereign Lord has given me an instructed tongue, to know the word that sustains the weary. He wakens me morning by morning, wakens my ear to listen like one being taught. The Sovereign Lord has opened my ears . . ." (Isaiah 50:4, 5, NIV).

Here we have the sense of someone actually learning from God every day, morning by morning. God can become our personal counselor when we listen carefully to His Word.

Psalm 119 is a personal testimony to that effect. "Your statutes are my delight; they are my counselors" (Psalm 119:24, NIV).

And the psalmist adds in verse 99: "I have more insight than all my teachers, for I meditate on your statutes" (Psalm 119:99, NIV).

Listening to the Word of God, meditating on it,

turns God into our personal counselor.

So listen. Try to listen in new ways. Let scenes from the Bible come alive in your mind. And try to listen actively.

Active listening also means that we apply what we hear to our own lives. In whatever type of study you do, always remember to end with application.

Ask yourself, "How does what I've heard apply to my problems, my challenges? How can I make these things real?" God invites us to follow new truths, radical truths. We may need to take courageous steps as Martin Luther once did when he followed the principles of God's Word instead of the traditions of a popular church.

Active listening to God's voice in Scripture is a skill that must be developed. It doesn't happen accidentally. It requires a definite commitment. Listening requires a definite place and a definite time. We need a quiet place where God's voice in the Bible can be distinguished from the noise around us and within us. We need time for the voice of God to sink in and to make a difference.

Looking at God

Now, let me tell you about the second important way in which our souls can be nurtured on a daily basis. After we listen, we need to look.

There's one admonition in the Bible that's vitally important when it comes to the care of the soul. It's a simple one we often overlook in our attempts to do religious things. The Bible urges us over and over to—seek God's face. And the great stories in the Bible are stories of people who responded.

Here's David, for example, in Psalm 27: "When You said, 'Seek My face,' my heart said to You, 'Your face, Lord, I will seek' " (Psalm 27:8, NKJV).

Our soul grows when it responds to this call to seek God Himself, to seek His face.

Another Psalm, exhorts us to: "Seek the Lord and His strength; seek His face evermore" (Psalm 105:4, NKJV).

Seek His face evermore, always.

Now, seeking God's face may sound like a pretty big order to fill. After all, the Almighty doesn't turn up around every corner. He is a Sovereign Being enthroned up in heaven.

But actually, Scripture shows us a very simple means of seeking God's face. That is, prayer. Prayer is a way of looking.

Generally, we view prayer as request time. We present our shopping list before the Almighty. We tell God how rough things are and ask Him to improve our situation.

It's certainly true that God is eager to meet our needs. Petitions are an important part of prayer. But there's another element that we've neglected. There is a vital aspect of prayer, probably the most important part, that has been lost in our cries for help.

And it is precisely this element of prayer that enables us to look—to catch a glimpse of the Almighty. Let's examine a few examples in the Bible of *looking* in prayer.

Did you know that David, more than any other person in Scripture, has left us a record of his prayers?

We can see many different prayers David made in many different circumstances throughout his life.

This record shows us that his prayers invariably included one thing—praise. It was praise that enabled him to consistently "seek God's face."

While serving in King Saul's court, David narrowly escaped the king's attempt to kill him. David had to flee for his life into the night. He became a fugitive. In his hour of desperation he sent up a plea to God, recorded in Psalm 59.

But his prayer was more than just a cry for help. It ended with these remarkable words of praise, recorded in Psalm 59: "But I will sing of Your power; yes, I will sing aloud of Your mercy in the morning; for You have been my defense and refuge in the day of my trouble" (Psalm 59:16, NKJV).

Perhaps the worst time of David's life occurred when his own son Absalom started a rebellion against him. He'd become an old man by this time. He was forced to flee from his palace, a fugitive once again.

In his despair, David cried out to God. But again, he managed to *look*, to praise. David said:

"But You, O Lord, are a shield for me, my glory and the One who lifts up my head" (Psalm 3:3, NKJV).

Praise was David's way of looking at God. This "man after God's own heart" knew how to seek God's face.

We need so very much to do the same. Praise, I believe, is the missing element in our prayer life. It can be the most important thing we do in our conversation with God. Praise transforms prayer into looking. And it is this focus on God that generates spiritual power that nurtures the soul.

Our prayers must become a way of looking. We need praise. That means that we must have a regular time for looking, just as we require a regular time for listening. Glimpses of God don't come casually. We must have more than a hurried petition before we rush out the door. Prayer must be more than a quick nod heavenward. If we want to see God, we must commit ourselves to take the time each day for devotional prayer.

Listening to God in His Word. Looking at God in prayer. This is how we develop a relationship that will nurture our souls. This is how God can become our Good Shepherd.

When life falls apart

Treena Kerr lived in a beautiful colonial mansion on Chesapeake Bay. She seemed to have just about everything. Her husband was the famous Galloping Gourmet on television—Graham Kerr. The couple had worked hard. They'd become very successful. They could afford a lavish lifestyle. They had wonderful friends.

But Treena was dying inside. The center wasn't holding. Those on the outside saw a cheery, glamorous woman. But those close to Treena knew she was struggling with serious emotional problems. In fact, she'd been going downhill for years.

At one point Treena had been judged incapable of managing her life. Doctors considered admitting her to a mental institution for an undetermined period. Only a high daily dose of Valium kept her going.

Fortunately, Treena had one more thing—a young maid named Ruthie who began praying for her. Ruthie told fellow believers at her tiny church and they began to pray for Treena too.

Ruthie knew everything else had failed the woman. Mr. Kerr had just taken her on a dream cruise around the world in a beautiful yacht to see if that would help. But she'd come home more miserable than ever.

One day, after three months of praying, Ruthie found Mrs. Kerr screaming at the ceiling in her bedroom. She got up enough courage to suggest, "Why don't you give your problems to God?"

Treena took up the challenge angrily. She shot back: "All right, God, if you're so clever, you deal with it, because I can't."

A week later she found herself in Ruthie's church. And before she knew it she was responding to an altar call. Treena knelt and began weeping: "I'm sorry, Jesus. Forgive me, Jesus," was all she could say.

Treena left that church feeling like God had touched her. Back home she started seeking that Good Shepherd. She started reading a Bible Ruthie had given her.

She kept reading until late into the night. Treena went to get her sleeping pills. But a little inner voice said, "You won't need anything like that anymore." So she took all her drugs and poured them down the bathroom sink.

Most people don't just quit that much Valium cold turkey, but Treena slept soundly and woke up refreshed, invigorated, and clear-eyed.

Treena kept listening to God in His Word. She kept

looking at Him in prayer.

A week later, Mr. Kerr returned from a trip to find his wife transformed. He thought her peace and kindness must have something to do with the season; it was Christmastime. But it lasted beyond the holidays.

For the next several weeks, Graham kept analyzing his wife. He'd known her since she was eleven. He had seen her slowly destroyed over the years. But now, he said, "She was totally put back together again, and really better and more loving than any time I could remember."

The woman falling apart had encountered something solid. She'd found a center for her life. She'd found a Good Shepherd. Even Treena's doctor confirmed it. "Your wife is a miracle," he told Graham with tears in his eyes. "I had never seen one, but now I have."

You can find a true center for your life right now. You can find a Good Shepherd who will nourish your soul. You can find green pastures and still waters.

God has laid out the essential steps of growth for us.

We need to listen carefully to Him in His Word. His voice must echo in our souls.

We need to look at Him carefully in prayer—praising Him and opening up our hearts to Him. It's His face that our souls must seek.

Are you ready to truly seek God in this way—every day?

Setting time aside for a devotional life is vital in the care and feeding of the human soul. God needs that time in order to work His wonders inside us. Won't you make a commitment to give him that time right now?

Two Scholars, One Murder

On the afternoon of November 1, 1991, police responded to a 911 call at Iowa State University. Entering a lecture room in Van Allen Hall, they found Professor Christoph Goertz slumped in his chair. He was bleeding from a gunshot wound to the back of his head.

They also found Professor Robert Smith sprawled on the floor, his chest stained with blood.

And they found three other murder victims.

Who had done this? Who had committed this outrage?

It turned out, incredibly enough, to be a graduate assistant at the university. A scholar who'd been disappointed. A scholar who'd been passed over. A scholar who had become consumed by revenge.

I want to tell you his story because it gives us an important picture of the human soul and how it can become distorted.

And I also want to tell you about another scholar, another man whose story is similar in several ways. This man shows us how the human soul can be healed.

The story of two scholars named Lu and Stephen offers stark contrasts in what can happen to a human soul in search of an identity. As we'll see, both had reasons to take revenge. They both could have been suspects. They both could have taken the path downward.

I want you to try to discover which one committed the crime, which one was the real murderer. Try to look for the clues.

We'll start with the scholar named Lu. He grew up in the residential compound of a military hospital. His mother was a doctor, his father a clerk. He was a quiet, timid child who loved to read.

In high school, Lu began to distinguish himself in math and physics and won a scholarship to a prestigious university.

It seemed things were going great for this young man. But underneath, Lu struggled with a wide streak of insecurity. He was short and unattractive and tried to make up for it by being smarter than everyone else. His friends got the impression he always needed to look down on other people. Lu seemed obsessed with getting money and recognition.

Now, let me tell you about the other scholar, Stephen.

He struggled with insecurity too. Stephen's parents divorced when he was a baby, and he grew up with two different families. One was wealthy, the other lower middle-class. One was basically Protestant, the other Catholic.

Stephen often felt like he didn't really fit in anywhere. He didn't belong.

To top it off, things were falling apart in the home where he spent most of his time. His mother and stepfather alternated between screaming fights and week-long silences. Sometimes Stephen had to act as the parent of his six younger brothers and sisters.

Like Lu, Stephen was a small kid. He developed late. And none of the pretty girls that he admired so intensely in school ever took an interest in him. Stephen was very bright and found school rather easy, but he just wasn't motivated to try very hard.

Lu and Stephen. Two intelligent young men. Two very insecure young men. Which one would turn out to be the murderer?

Let's go forward a few years to their time of crisis.

For Lu, it happened after he began working on his doctoral dissertation. He was doing research in the field of ionization. Lu had always done brilliantly on written exams. But he struggled with research. And his own roommate, a physics student named Shan, was showing him up. Shan's work was a stunning success. Lu began to feel resentful.

And then came the oral exam. He had to defend his thesis before a group of professors. Lu bombed out. He couldn't answer many of the questions his department chairman kept asking. The young man felt he'd been humiliated.

Shortly afterward, Lu was passed over for a coveted prize in the physics department.

To top it off, Lu just couldn't seem to find a job

anywhere. He applied all over the country, but money for physics research projects was hard to come by.

Lu felt he had to do something.

Now, let's take a look at the other scholar, Stephen, and his time of crisis. It happened after he'd already begun to teach courses in philosophy as a replacement for other professors on leave. Stephen had proved to be a very popular teacher. Everyone at the university seemed to like his work.

But then a financial crunch hit the school. Administrators decided the philosophy department would have to be cut back. Who would they let go?

The president of the school met with faculty members and announced the decision. Stephen would not be rehired.

He got the news at his home. Impulsively, Stephen decided to go and see the president. He wasn't quite ready to bow to the inevitable. This was his dream job. This was what he'd been working for most of his life.

But after a thirty-minute meeting, the president said he was very sorry but they just couldn't keep him on.

Stephen had a wife and two young children to support. And the bad news had come just two days before Christmas.

It didn't seem fair. Stephen felt he had to do something.

Well, there we have it. Two scholars. One in physics, the other in philosophy. Both were bitterly disappointed. Both had a motive for striking back. Who would turn into a murderer?

Stephen had come from a dysfunctional family.

He'd always struggled to fit in.

Lu had come from a more normal family. But he struggled with insecurity too. He always felt people were conspiring against him.

The challenge these two men faced is really a challenge that comes to most of us. How do we build a healthy identity, a healthy soul, when our past has damaged our hearts? How do we build a healthy soul, when our environment is pushing us down?

Any talk about the care and feeding of the human soul has to deal with this problem. It's at the foundation of healthy development.

When we don't get a healthy dose of love early on in life, something happens to our souls. They're like sponges that dry out and harden. Our capacity to receive love is affected.

And so later, even when a spouse or a friend pours love in; it's not really absorbed. Even when your life is filled with nice things and status symbols, it's never enough. Affirmation doesn't become a part of you. It seems to go right through you.

Lu and Stephen both struggled with insecurity. They struggled with fitting in, with finding a place. Both of their souls could have become hardened. And yet, when the crisis came, they actually reacted in opposite ways. One became a murderer. One went on to become a respected professor.

Why? I believe we find a key turning point in their lives some time before the crisis hit. It happened when they were confronted with love. Their responses sent them down two very different paths.

Lu encountered love through a pastor who befriended him. Tom Miller headed a Bible Fellowship group on the campus. He would often take Lu and a few other students, who had no vehicles, in his van to a discount grocery store. He also gathered a group for Bible study.

Pastor Miller talked about how God demonstrated His love for us. He shared texts like Isaiah 44:2 where God declares that He is the One who formed us in the womb.

And Psalm 139 tells us, we are: " . . . fearfully and wonderfully made" (Psalm 139:14, NKJV).

God has an interest in each individual life that He has created. We are called the "apple of His eye" in Zechariah 2:8. Jesus said in Matthew 10:30 that the very hairs on our head are numbered.

Pastor Miller tried to get across the truth that the apostle John communicated so enthusiastically in 1 John: "Behold what manner of love the Father has bestowed on us, that we should be called children of God!" (1 John 3:1, NKJV).

Lu's friends listened. A couple of the physics students decided to commit their lives to Christ. But Lu just couldn't get interested. He didn't grasp the love of God. He didn't relate it to the hardening of his soul. He was too busy trying to earn recognition, trying to make other people acknowledge how smart he was. Accepting the gift of grace seemed insulting.

When Lu's friends would talk to him about their personal relationship with Christ, he became defensive. He'd challenge them, asking, "OK, show me what God looks like."

Stephen, the other scholar, encountered love through two UCLA football players. While still in high school, he'd been invited to hear them speak at a local church. The two athletes shared their stories of how they'd met Christ and explained what the gospel is all about.

They talked about the cost of God's love, the sacrifice God made. He loved the world so much that He gave His only begotten Son. And this Son has a wonderful plan for each one of us. He came "that they may have life, and that they may have it more abundantly" (John 10:10, NKJV).

Stephen had the sense that they were talking directly to him. The grace of Christ seemed aimed straight at that hollow place inside, that emptiness, that lack of belonging anywhere.

So Stephen began to grow in that relationship with Christ. He was fascinated by this unique individual and began to read about Him constantly.

As Stephen himself put it, "I found in Christ rest for my soul—a place to stop, a person to be, a family to which to belong, a true home in which to live."

Two scholars. Two young men struggling with insecurity. One found a way out by embracing love. The other couldn't stop trying to earn it.

I'm sure you know by now which man became the murderer. Lu's crisis led him into a terrible killing spree at the University of Iowa. He'd been humiliated by his professor. He'd been turned down for a coveted prize. Somebody had to pay.

Lu was still trying to MAKE people respect and admire him. He hadn't let go of his twisted sense of superiority.

In one of his last letters he wrote, "I have sworn to myself that I would take revenge at any cost."

Lu purchased a .38 caliber revolver at a local sporting-goods store, mailed some money he'd saved back home, and walked into Van Allen Hall on that November afternoon in 1991 to kill five human beings.

Afterward he turned the gun on himself.

It matters how we deal with our insecurities. It matters how we deal with the dark emotions that sometimes threaten to strangle us. All this determines the shape of our souls.

Not all insecure people go on to commit murder, of course. But they can spend their whole lives trying to control and manipulate others into meeting their needs.

All of us have been hurt in one way or another. All of us have that deep longing for love and for healing. But we can't MAKE other people give us what we need. We can't manipulate others into respecting us more. We can't ever work hard enough to fill the emptiness. We can never get enough inside that way. We can't earn love.

That always backfires. Sometimes it backfires in terrible ways.

You can only work on one thing—*you* and *your* ability to take in the good stuff, your capacity to absorb love. And there's only one reason we can hope to do that. God can work on the state of our hearts.

He gives us this wonderful promise in Ezekiel: "I will give you a new heart and put a new spirit within you; I will take the heart of stone out of your flesh and give you a heart of flesh" (Ezekiel 36:26, NKJV).

God can deal with that heart of stone, that dry sponge that has become hardened, that can't take in love in a healthy way. God can give us a heart of flesh, a heart that responds to positive regard and affirmation.

That's the area where you can work successfully: your capacity to absorb. It's not what happened to you; it's not how other people are treating you that's messing up your life. It's what you choose to take in, what you build on, that counts.

The New Testament emphasizes the receiving end, what we take in from God. That's how real healing happens.

Listen to Paul in Ephesians: "I pray that out of his glorious riches he may strengthen you with power through his Spirit in your inner being, so that Christ may dwell in your hearts through faith. And I pray that you, being rooted and established in love, may have power . . . to grasp how wide and long and high and deep is the love of Christ, and to know this love that surpasses knowledge—that you may be filled to the measure of all the fullness of God" (Ephesians 3:16-19, NIV).

How do you get filled up; how do you get enough in. By learning to grasp more of the positive, instead of harping on the negative. By learning to absorb God's love and expand in it. To be filled, you've got to grasp.

The only way we can be filled up is to work on the receiving end. We can't keep blaming others. We can't keep focusing on the bad things people have done to us. We've got to focus on our own capacity to absorb love.

That's exactly what Stephen, the other scholar, did. He became fascinated by the person of Christ. He couldn't read enough about Him in the gospels. He absorbed this person's qualities into his life.

Do you know what Stephen did more than anything else? He just admired. He learned to admire and appreciate Christ.

That's what Jesus commended a woman named Mary for one evening in Bethany. Her sister, Martha, was scurrying around the house preparing supper for Christ and His disciples. Mary was sitting at Jesus' feet, listening to Him with rapt attention. Martha tried to make her feel guilty for not helping out.

But Jesus told busy Martha that she was worried about too many things. Mary had chosen the one thing that was most important, and that wouldn't be taken from her.

She was just admiring. She was just taking in Christ's love. She wasn't trying to earn it.

That's what Stephen writes about the most in telling his story. He describes how he came to admire Christ's charisma, His mysterious power, His skill in transforming all kinds of individuals.

Stephen's eyes were opened—wider and wider. He began to grasp the height and depth of Christ's love. He absorbed it. And that hard sponge inside him began to soften; the emptiness began to fill up.

So how did Stephen react during his crisis?

Well, after the president confirmed the bad news,

Stephen went back home and celebrated Christmas with his family. He knew many students had been praying that he'd stay on. But he felt he'd tried his best and could leave the matter in God's hands.

What Stephen didn't know was that the president of the school just couldn't sleep that night. He kept wondering if he'd done the right thing. And sometime in the middle of the night, he decided that he'd find some way to keep Stephen on as a philosophy teacher.

Stephen was, of course, overjoyed when he got the good news. He hadn't tried to make anyone feel guilty about firing him. He hadn't tried to force anyone to acknowledge his great accomplishments. The reversal of fortune had come to him as an act of providence. It was a gift. He knew where he belonged.

Today, Dr. Stephen Davis is a respected author and professor, teaching philosophy and religion at that same school, Claremont McKenna College in California.

Two scholars. Two young men struggling with insecurity. One tried to get recognition by manipulation and by force. One received love as a gift.

That's the only way we can receive it. That's the only way we can become whole human beings. That's the only way our souls can start to take healthy shape.

How is the state of your soul today? What are you struggling with? Does it sometimes seem like you'll never fill up that emptiness? It's time to stop trying to earn it. It's time to stop trying to make other people give you what you need.

It's time to sit at Jesus' feet. We've got to accept

love as a gift from God. We need that love poured out in our hearts.

Will you open yourself up to that experience right now?

Feeding the Soul

Chuck gets out of his hot car and walks up to his buddy Pat's house.

In his book *Touch Me if You Dare*, Patrick Donadio describes a memorable incident from his life in a gang called "The Rubes."

Chuck knocks on the door. Pat comes out.

"You ready?"

Pat raised his eyebrows, "Ready for what?"

"To rob the bakery at Fourth and Elm," Chuck replies, grinning.

Pat walks out onto the porch remembering uncomfortably.

Chuck gestures, a little miffed that his buddy seems to be clueless.

"You know, we planned it like two weeks ago."

Pat tries to change the subject, "Where's Fred these days?"

Chuck replies impatiently, "He went upstate to visit his new girlfriend."

After an awkward silence, Pat begins to explain hesitantly.

"Chuck, a few days ago something happened to me."

"What happened?"

"I got saved."

"Saved from what?"

"I accepted Christ as my Saviour. I went forward in a church service, confessed my sins, and I think I've found peace and forgiveness."

Chuck looks out across the lawn for a moment, and then back at his buddy.

"OK, so now you're saved. Big deal! Come on, let's go rob that bakery!" He walks down the steps.

For some people, "getting your soul saved" doesn't seem to be such a big deal—when it comes to actual behavior. They separate religion from real life.

And that's a problem for more of us than we like to think. How does all the "soul talk" about faith and grace and spirit-filled living actually make a difference in our day-to-day existence?

In this book, we're reading about the care and nurture of the human soul. We're looking at healthy ways of nurturing spirituality.

And, in this chapter, I'd like to tackle a very serious challenge. How do we make sure that Soul Care really makes a difference in our everyday lives?

In the last chapter, we talked about developing a healthy relationship with God. How do we make sure that our relationship with Him actually affects our behavior?

In this chapter, we're going to talk about the way we grow. But I don't want to just give you some nice slogans on the care and feeding of the soul. I don't want to just lay out some spiritual fast food. I'd like to offer some very practical instruction from the Bible.

I believe we need divine insight on this subject. We need it because human beings have gone on an awful lot of detours in search of their souls. They've hit a lot of dead ends.

In ages past, sincere people starved themselves in desert caves or sat on top of high pillars for years—trying to care for their souls.

More recently, people have taken to wearing crystals and chanting magical formulas and channeling spirit beings—all to nourish their souls.

I don't believe that all so-called spiritual food is created equal. There are things that truly nourish our souls and things that leave it empty. There are healthy and unhealthy ways to pursue spirituality. Some kinds of religion help us experience intimacy with God. Other kinds of religion leave us guilty, manipulated, and repressed.

I'd like us to focus on healthy ways to care for our souls, healthy ways to nourish our souls.

I want to concentrate on two ways we generally go about trying to feed our souls. One way involves taking things out. The other way involves putting things in.

Let's look first at something Jesus said about the kingdom of heaven as it's recorded in the book of Matthew: "The kingdom of heaven is like treasure hidden in a field, which a man found and hid; and for joy over it he goes and sells all that he has and buys that field" (Matthew 13:44, NKJV).

Here we have a man getting rid of his worldly possessions. He sells everything. Why? In order to avoid the love of money? In order to make a big sacrifice? No, he wants very badly to get this hidden treasure; it's worth selling out for. In his joy he goes out and sells all he has.

Jesus makes the same point in His parable about the pearl of great price. A wise merchant sells everything he has to get that pearl. Why? Because it's worth everything he has.

There's a lesson here about the kingdom of heaven, about the care of our souls. We successfully get rid of the bad stuff in our lives by pursuing something good, something better. We find a treasure and so we get rid of anything that gets in the way of possessing that treasure.

Unfortunately, many people get stuck in the process of throwing out the bad stuff. They lose sight of hidden treasure. They just keep trying to get rid of more and more "worldly" things in their lives. They concentrate on suppressing lust and anger and envy and pride. They keep hoping that getting rid of negative emotions will nourish their souls.

In other words, some people see the care and feeding of the soul as primarily a matter of getting the bad stuff out. The soul is supposed to grow in the vacuum that results. Unfortunately, something else usually happens.

Jesus once told a parable about an evil spirit that had been cast out of a man. After wandering through desolate places, the spirit gets an idea: " 'I will return to my house from which I came.' And when he comes, he finds it empty, swept, and put in order.

Then he goes and takes with him seven other spirits more wicked than himself, and they enter and dwell there; and the last state of that man is worse than the first" (Matthew 12:44, 45, NKJV).

The spirit comes back and finds the house empty, the soul of the man is empty. Oh it's clean; it's swept and put in order. But there's nothing occupying the center of his life. So what happens in this vacuum? More evil spirits come in. More compulsions. More negative emotions. The man is in worse shape now than before he started cleaning up his act.

Do you know what happens when we just zero in on getting rid of the bad? The bad takes center stage in our minds. We're thinking about not lusting or not getting angry or not getting depressed. We're frowning at those enemies, pointing our finger at them, determined to avoid them. But it's still lust and anger and depression that remain the focus of attention.

And they'll be right back as soon as we let our guard down. They'll be right back, stronger than ever, because we've been looking at them for so long, trying to stare them down for so long.

Our souls are going to remain very dry as long as *avoidance* is at the center of our religion. We may appear to be very upright, very holy, but our souls can be withering away inside us. Negative emotions will never nourish our souls. We need hidden treasure to nourish our souls.

I can't think of a more vivid example of this than the parents of a good friend of mine. His recollection of these two opposite individuals sticks with me. We'll call them Sherman and Tracy.

My friend's father, Sherman, had been, before his conversion, a rowdy young man given to drink. Sherman was proud that he'd given up everything— drinking, smoking, worldly places of amusement— just like that. He was going to serve God if it killed him.

And Sherman had faithfully avoided these things for six decades. He practiced the religion of avoidance. He followed the rules of his church; he kept himself uncorrupted by the world. He even boasted that he'd never let any unhealthy food pass through his lips.

But Sherman did let some very unkind words pass through those lips. He often criticized other church members for not being as strict as he was. He sometimes verbally abused his wife unmercifully.

This man could say No to all kinds of things. But he had a hard time saying Yes to kindness or grace.

As my friend looks back, he has a painful recollection of never really touching his father's soul, never really receiving love and nurture.

But Tracy was a very different story. My friend's voice softens when he talks about his mother. She overflowed with compassion and love. Her faith was much simpler than her husband's. She was sustained by the fact that "Jesus loves me, this I know."

Tracy befriended all kinds of people through the years. She once took a young, pregnant girl who'd just moved into town under her wing and helped her get a job and a place to stay. Sometimes she took in drunks. Decades later, recovering alcoholics would recall her as the most beautiful person they'd ever known.

Tracy's life centered around grace. Her life of service seemed effortless. She wasn't defined by the things she avoided. She was defined by the positive qualities she expressed.

Sherman and Tracy are opposites in my friend's recollection. They show us two very different ways of trying to care for the soul.

One way just tries to clean up the house, leaving it empty. The other way pursues hidden treasure.

One way is ruled by quantities, the things it avoids.

The other way is nourished by qualities it pursues.

Friends, our souls can only be nourished by positive qualities. Nothing else will do. Trying to have less anger, less lust, less envy won't fill us up. Something bigger, something stronger, something greater needs to drive those negative emotions out.

Here's Paul's suggestion in Galatians: "The fruit of the Spirit is love, joy, peace, longsuffering, kindness, goodness, faithfulness, gentleness, self-control" (Galatians 5:22, 23, NKJV).

These are the things we need in the center of our lives. These are the things that must characterize our religion. These are the things that nourish our souls.

Paul offers us a wonderful summary of soul care toward the end of his letter to the Philippians: "Finally, brethren, whatever things are true, whatever things are noble, whatever things are just, whatever things are pure, whatever things are lovely, whatever things are of good report, if there is any virtue and if there is anything praiseworthy—meditate on these things" (Philippians 4:8, NKJV).

Fill your mind with what is noble and lovely and true. Fill your mind with God's qualities. Fill your mind with His grace and love.

Negative emotions don't yield to willpower. We can't just make them leave by frowning hard enough. They always come back in some way—stronger than before. Only positive emotions can drive them out. Pursuing hidden treasure is the best way of getting rid of the bad. We need something filling up our souls in order to push out whatever is threatening our souls.

Let me tell you how a young man named Richard discovered that principle. Richard had a problem. It was pornography. And he knew that this problem might ruin his marriage. He'd fallen into the habit of sneaking home with certain videos once in awhile. These illicit sexual images had become addictive.

Once, Richard's wife had caught him with the materials. She felt terribly hurt, of course, and she felt humiliated. Her husband was fulfilling his sexual fantasies elsewhere—with other women on videotape. She wondered if there was something wrong with her.

Richard felt terrible too. He told his wife he was very sorry. He claimed that this was a unique incident.

But the habit had dug in. Richard found himself falling again and again—into pornography.

Well, Richard prayed about his problem. He prayed very hard that he would not be overcome by lust. He found verses in the Bible that warned of the sins of the flesh and the deceitfulness of the eye. Richard prayed hard *against* pornography. He tried to stomp that sin out of his life.

And yet sometimes, he would get up from his knees, after praying earnestly for an hour, and fall for the same old sin. That was deeply distressing. He wondered why God wasn't rescuing him. He was fighting so hard against temptation.

Well, on one occasion, Richard's wife left for a trip across country to visit her family. She was going to be gone for almost a month. Richard knew he would be tempted. He knew he had a battle on his hands.

But on the morning following his wife's departure, Richard ran across some wonderful verses in the psalms on praise. And he felt inspired to praise God, to raise a new song to the Almighty Himself. Richard thanked God for the goodness of life, for His many acts of providence, and he praised God for His tireless patience, His transforming power, His matchless grace.

Looking out the window of his bedroom on a bright, new morning, Richard felt God expanding in his heart. God was becoming very real as he praised Him.

All through that day, Richard found himself enjoying God's companionship. And at the end of the day he realized he hadn't been fighting against lust at all. He hadn't been struggling to get those pornographic images out of his mind.

Something else had taken their place. God had simply become bigger, more vivid.

Throughout that long month, Richard continued this kind of positive prayer. And he never fell for the same old sin. He'd found something better. He'd found a better way to fight. It was the good fight of faith. Not the old fight against sin. He wasn't focused on lust. He wasn't frowning at it and pointing at it and quoting verses against it.

He had changed his focus of attention. Looking in God's direction had given him momentum.

The pull of the old habit didn't disappear forever, of course. Richard would still be tempted on occasion. But now his prayers were very different. He focused on positive qualities: what he wanted to pursue, not just what he wanted to avoid. And that kind of fight proved to be sustainable. He could push pornography out of his life because he was pursuing something better.

It's very important for us to understand that soul care is about expanding our lives. It's not just about cutting life down to proper size. Soul is not what we have left over after everything else is eliminated.

No, healthy religion is expansive. It expands our hearts and minds.

Let's look again at what Jesus said the kingdom of heaven is like. "The kingdom of heaven is like a mustard seed, which a man took and sowed in his field, which indeed is the least of all the seeds; but when it is grown it is greater than the herbs and becomes a tree, so that the birds of the air come and nest in its branches" (Matthew 13:31, 32, NKJV).

The tiny seed expands under the broad sky, growing into a plant so large that birds can nest in its branches.

The more we concentrate on the essential seed, on

knowing God, the more expansive our soul life becomes. The less we concentrate on knowing God, the more constricted our soul life becomes.

The apostle Paul certainly knew what to concentrate on. That's why He could testify so eloquently about the "surpassing greatness" of knowing Jesus as his Lord. That's why all his previous honors and accomplishments seemed like rubbish in comparison.

So we need to ask ourselves a question. What best characterizes our attempts to nourish our souls? Are we primarily pursuing, or primarily avoiding? Are we seeking to know Christ, or trying to stare down sin?

God doesn't want our faith to shrink us into avoidance or pettiness. He wants to expand our lives with His positive qualities.

Caring for the soul isn't about putting square pegs in square holes. It's about expanding; it's about "growing into the whole measure of all the fullness of Christ."

Life is so much more beautiful when we have something positive, something wonderful to pursue in our lives. It ennobles everything we do.

Why not begin a healthy kind of soul care right now? God wants to broaden your life with the fruit of the Spirit. He wants us to nurture that good tree spreading its branches against the sky.

You may have struggled with negative emotions for a long, long time. You may be locked in a losing battle against habits that dominate you.

Why not try the good fight of faith? Turn your attention to God and allow Him to begin building good emotions in your heart. Focus on His love and joy and peace. Fix your mind on all that He has for you, all that is true and noble and praiseworthy. Let's begin that process right now.

Seeing Through God's Eyes

He was a hard-nosed fanatic, a man whose religion had made him violent and intolerant. He set out down this road on a journey as a zealous persecutor.

But he would never come back—as the same man.

This persecutor somehow became a gifted encourager, one of the most loving religious leaders of all time. His remarkable transformation shows us how we can become whole in relationships with others.

A brilliant young Pharisee named Saul believed he was on a mission from God. He'd become an expert at interpreting the laws of Jewish religious tradition. He was positive he had the truth and nothing but the truth, and he just knew that everybody else outside his group was mixed up, especially a certain sect which followed Jesus.

They claimed He was the Messiah. Saul vowed to destroy this heresy. He tracked down believers and had them dragged off to prison. One day, he set off toward the city of Damascus, determined to hunt down followers of Jesus there.

But something happened to him on the road to Damascus. A bright light knocked him to his knees. Something supernatural had happened.

Saul asked, "Who are you, Lord?"

A voice answered, "I am Jesus, whom you are persecuting."

Suddenly, Saul had to confront the fact that he'd been persecuting the Lord of the universe. Blinded and helpless, he had to rely on the very people he'd tried to destroy to lead him to Christ.

In the weeks and months that followed, Saul the fanatic acquired a radical new perspective. He had to discard his old prejudices. He had to see people through new eyes.

You catch this new perspective in every one of Paul's epistles. You can see it in how he greets believers, how he encourages and nurtures them. Paul is constantly thanking God for the wonderful qualities he sees in the people he meets. His soul is constantly broadened because he catches glimpses of God's grace in the faces around him.

A big part of becoming a whole human being involves forming healthy relationships. Our souls are nurtured by healthy relationships. Our spiritual life is broadened.

That's what we're going to look at in this chapter. How do we become healthier in the way we relate to others?

Paul obviously found a big answer to this question. Paul the intolerant fanatic acquired a radical new perspective that transformed his relationships. It's a perspective that can transform our relationships with other people.

Look at how Paul expresses it in Romans: "Accept one another, then, just as Christ accepted you, in order to bring praise to God" (Romans 15:7, NIV).

How can we become more accepting of others? How can we break down barriers that divide us? By understanding how Christ accepts us. He accepts us as His beloved children, despite our weaknesses. Because He accepts us freely, we can extend that same grace to others.

Every human being has great value because Christ loves them, because Christ has died for them. And Christ's love compels us to look at people as God does. That's the perspective that can transform our relationship—seeing through God's eyes.

Here's Paul again, expanding on the theme in Ephesians: "And be kind to one another, tenderhearted, forgiving one another, just as God in Christ also forgave you" (Ephesians 4:32, NKJV).

How can we become more forgiving? How can we prevent anger from seeping down inside us and turning into bitterness? By plugging into the fact that God has forgiven us so generously. We can release others from our condemnation because God has released us from His. We forgive because we are forgiven.

Jesus Himself laid down the same kind of principle in His last discourse to His disciples. He said: "A new command I give you: Love one another. As I have loved you, so you must love one another" (John 13:34, NIV).

Jesus is saying, "Love one another with the love I have given you."

Do you see the pattern here in the New Testament?

Accept one another as God accepts us.

Forgive one another as God forgives us.

Love one another as God loves us.

That's how it works. That's how we can start building healthy relationships with others.

We need a healthy relationship with God first! We need His input in our lives. We will never really be able to value others until we know in our hearts how much God values us.

So it's important to build our relationships with others on the basis of the love, acceptance, and forgiveness that we receive from God.

Let's look at a few examples of how we can do that, how we overcome obstacles between people.

Our most common problems revolve around personality differences. Some people tend to be introspective. Other people tend to be outgoing. Some individuals are laid back. Others are very driven.

We're all different. Unfortunately, we tend to react negatively to those who are opposite in temperament.

For example, let's say there are two roommates, Sarah and Kathy. Sarah tends to be spontaneous. Kathy tends to be controlled.

One evening, Sarah breezes in and exclaims, "Let's throw a party and invite some people over tonight!"

Kathy throws up her hands. Things like this have to be planned ahead of time. She has to have everything organized; even the cans in the kitchen cabinets are arranged alphabetically. She tells Sarah this is a horrible idea.

Well, Sarah wants her roommate to lighten up, to live a little. But the more surprises Sarah pulls, the more controlled Kathy becomes. And the more controlled Kathy becomes, the more spontaneous Sarah tries to be to make up for it.

Each person is trying to correct the other person's extreme. But they end up just reacting against each other. They end up even more extreme. And they end up talking past each other.

"You're so scatterbrained and disorganized."

"You're incredibly uptight."

But the interesting fact is this: both of these people need to move toward the center. Kathy needs to become a little more spontaneous. Sarah needs to be a little more organized.

So really, Sarah and Kathy need each other; they could learn from each other. Unfortunately, human nature tends to react against opposites. And so it's very easy to push each other farther and farther apart.

But, when we see each other as God does, we get a different perspective. God's love and acceptance and forgiveness change the picture. He's the One who created all these different personalities. And God doesn't make junk. We can't just write off people who are different from us. They have value. They have potential. They have something to teach us.

When we look at others from God's perspective, we can learn from them, not just react to them. Sometimes the people who are most different from us have the most to teach us.

We can learn so much—when we look at people from God's perspective.

But let's say your problems with someone are deeper than just differences in personality. Let's say you're having serious conflicts with someone at work, maybe someone at home. How does God's acceptance and love and forgiveness work in these cases? Can it really make a practical difference?

Well, let's look at one of the major contributors to our quarrels and misunderstandings. Do you know what lies behind the vast majority of interpersonal conflicts? The win-lose mentality. That's the assumption that, whenever there's a problem between two people, one of us is going to win, and the other lose. One of us must come out on top.

People with a win-lose attitude turn every little disagreement into a big battle. Every misunderstanding is a major threat. Every conflict has to be fought to the bitter end.

A win-lose attitude pushes people to defend turf instead of finding common ground, to score points instead of resolving issues, to prove they are right instead of trying to understand.

Why do we fall into this trap? Usually because it's so much easier to fight that problem out there, than to deal with the problem in here. If anger or bitterness smolder inside us, if we're struggling with negative emotions, then it's much easier to blame them on an enemy than to deal with the emotions themselves.

But let's look at a healthy alternative to the win-lose attitude. There's an interesting case study in conflict resolution that comes to us from the Bible. It revolves around a character named Jonathan, the son of King Saul.

Saul had become insanely jealous of a young warrior named David. David had been anointed by the prophet Samuel to be the next king. So Saul adopted a familiar attitude. It's either you or me—this kingdom isn't big enough for both of us. He spent a lot of his time chasing David all over the Judean countryside, trying to eliminate him as a challenger.

Saul's son, Jonathan, could easily have adopted his father's win-lose perspective. After all, *he* was the prince who should have inherited his father's throne. But instead of concluding that the kingdom wasn't big enough for him and David, Jonathan did something else. He looked at God's covenant, God's plan for Israel. And he decided that God's covenant was wide enough for both of them.

Jonathan and David made their own separate peace, their own separate covenant together. It's recorded in First Samuel. Jonathan made this pledge: "And the Lord be with you as He has been with my father. And you shall not only show me the kindness of the Lord while I still live, . . . you shall not cut off your kindness from my house forever" (1 Samuel 20:13-15, NKJV).

Jonathan concentrated on a plan that would be good for both him and David. He looked for the best solution in a difficult situation. In other words, he had a win-win attitude. Both of us can win—if our aim is to serve God.

Whenever we find ourselves in a conflict we have to remember one thing: God wants both of us to win. God loves both of us. God wants the best for both of us. He doesn't have to love one less in order to love the other more.

God's love is wide enough and deep enough to take in all our needs. So when we have that love inside us we can extend it to others. We can adopt a win-win attitude.

You can sense this in the epistles of Paul, the persecutor who became a great encourager. Take his letters to believers in Corinth for example. These people were struggling with all kinds of problems. Believers were suing each other. Some were even involved in incest. Many were criticizing Paul's leadership.

It would have been easy for Paul, the great apostle, to put these people down in order to build up his credentials. He could have written them off because of their rebellious attitude.

Instead, Paul appealed to their conscience as a tender father. He pled with them to face their moral problems squarely. And then he wrote these remarkable words: "I do not say this to condemn; for I have said before that you are in our hearts, to die together and to live together" (2 Corinthians 7:3, NKJV).

Paul was animated by God's grace. He was compelled by Christ's love. And so, even in the midst of serious conflict with Corinthian believers, he wanted the best for them; he wanted them to win. He tried to find solutions. His letters to the Corinthians are full of that spirit.

We need a win-win attitude in all our conflicts.

That's how we resolve them; that's how we avoid turning every disagreement into a major battle. A win-win attitude focuses on solutions instead of on how to score points. You don't withdraw and pout, you don't try to manipulate, you focus on solutions.

Counselors often suggest three specific steps we can use to turn quarrels into a dialogue aimed at solutions.

First, separate the person from the problem. Don't attack the other person. Don't say "You always" or "You never." Isolate the problem you want to fix.

Second, focus on interests, not positions. That is, instead of just defending your position, your side of the matter, look at what needs you are both trying to meet. What do each of you really want?

Third, think of options that benefit both of you. Brainstorm possible solutions that meet your needs.

For example, let's say one spouse wants the window open at night. The other wants the window closed. People can build a long conflict around these two positions. Is a half-opened window the only answer?

Well, look at the needs. One person wants fresh air; one person wants warmth. Maybe buying an electric blanket—and keeping the window open, would satisfy both.

You can win-win much more of the time than you think, if you just concentrate on solutions, instead of trying to come out the victor, instead of trying to make the other person lose. Sometimes all it takes is one person coming up with a gracious answer to a problem.

Rodney Roberson was working at a homeless shelter to pay his way through seminary. He could tell it was going to be a bad night. It was very cold and raining hard. Soon all the cots and sleeping mats were taken. But the street people still kept coming in. Arguments broke out everywhere. People were cursing angrily. Some began to fight over sleeping mats.

In the midst of this tension, a large man named José stumbled in and threw down his sleeping mat. After managing to yank off his boots, he collapsed in a drunken stupor. The stench from José's feet quickly filled the air. People nearby insisted Rodney do something about it—immediately.

Well, the obvious solution seemed to be to persuade José to take a shower. But Rodney couldn't rouse him. He was breathing, but seemed dead to the world. Rodney and two coworkers discussed hauling the man to the shower; but he weighed more than two hundred pounds.

Some of the street people demanded that Rodney drag José back out to the sidewalk. But others howled in protest. It seemed that, for anyone to win, someone had to lose.

But then, Rodney got an idea—why not bring the shower to José? He found a wash basin and some lemon-scented dish-washing liquid. Then he knelt down by the drunken man and began to peel off his filthy socks. The stench was almost overwhelming.

But for several minutes, Rodney scrubbed José's feet with a soapy washcloth. He carefully dried them with a towel. Suddenly, he noticed he was surrounded by people. Rodney stood up warily and looked around.

Everyone was grinning at him—even the ones who'd been complaining the loudest. In fact, people he'd never seen smile before were grinning. Men and women of all races. One woman stepped forward with tears in her eyes, took Rodney's soapy hands and kissed them.

A quiet hush had fallen over the place. There would be no more shouting or threats that night. People with sleeping mats gave to someone without one. The conflict was over. It had been washed away by someone who didn't need to take sides, someone who didn't need to score points, someone willing to be, like Jesus, chief among them by becoming a servant.

When we have God's love in our lives, God's acceptance and forgiveness in our lives, we can resolve conflicts. When we know how God values us, then we can value others.

We can learn from people—instead of just reacting to them.

We can turn conflicts from win-lose, to win-win.

It all starts with a healthy relationship with the God who cherishes us. It all starts with understanding how wide and deep God's love really is.

Let's decide to adopt Paul's perspective right now. God has made the ultimate sacrifice so that all of us can win. Christ's love can compel us, can move us. Let's determine that His acceptance and forgiveness will start to shape all our relationships.

Let's start resolving our conflicts from God's point

of view. We can become stronger—and we can become more loving at the same time. We can break down every barrier with the grace that God pours into our hearts.

Body and Soul

Of all the places you might think of going—to learn how to better take care of your spiritual life—the gym is probably not one of them.

And yet a healthier body may be one thing your worn out soul needs the most.

There's a long tradition in the Christian church of people abusing their bodies as a way of caring for their souls.

An Egyptian peasant named Antony was one of the first. He came to be regarded as a saint for living nearly ninety years alone in the desert. One of his claims to fame was that he never changed his clothes or washed his face.

Then there was Simon Stylites. He took the denial of the body to new heights. Living alone out in the desert wasn't enough. He built a platform sixty feet in the air and lived there for thirty-seven years, dressed in animal skins and preaching to pilgrims who came to see him.

A hermit named Makarios of Alexandria also became legendary. During one fast, he remained in a corner of his cell without speaking or moving for forty days. He permitted himself to eat only some raw cabbage on Sundays.

When a devout woman named Paula founded a monastic community in the Holy Land, she gave her nuns this advice: "A clean body and clean clothes betoken an unclean mind." Paula slept on the ground and never bathed unless dangerously ill.

Somehow many believers got it into their heads that the body and the soul were enemies, that you could only care for one at the expense of the other. The need for self-control was turned into an obsession with self-denial.

Christian ascetics thought that if they abused their physical self enough, then their spiritual self would become strong. They wanted to free the soul from the entrapment of the body.

There are not many desert hermits around these days. At least the Christian church doesn't treat them as celebrities. Most of us don't go around whipping ourselves in penitence; we don't wall ourselves up in a cave in order to find God.

But this idea of the soul and the body as enemies persists; it lingers in the back of our minds. We separate the spiritual from the physical. We instinctively feel that if we want to be truly spiritual, we shouldn't pay too much attention to the body and its needs.

In this chapter, I'd like to suggest that the body and the soul are more closely tied together than you've probably imagined. We need to look at ourselves as a whole, a whole with interrelated dimensions, as God created us: spirit, mind, and body.

I'd like to demonstrate that caring for our bodies properly can actually help us better care for our souls. Yes, that's right, physical health can have an impact on our spiritual health.

Now maybe you've heard about a similar, related principle. Maybe you've heard about the research that indicates that spiritual health, peace of mind, can help us overcome disease, can help us defeat chronic illnesses. Perhaps you know about the connection from that angle: spiritual health affects physical health.

But, I want to show you how it works the other way, how physical health can impact our spiritual health. We're going to look closely at that particular aspect of ourselves as whole human beings.

Why is caring for our bodies an important element in spiritual health? Here's the first reason. A healthy body helps us have a clearer mind.

To be specific, our diet, the things we eat, can influence our thoughts, our feelings, our behavior. New scientific findings are beginning to suggest that there is a subtle relationship between diet and mental health.

Dr. U. D. Register headed the School of Health at Loma Linda University for many years. He's been a guest on our program. And he's put together a great deal of evidence on this subject.

Dr. Register points out that we now have documented evidence that certain vitamin deficiencies, for example, can damage the nervous system and cause mental disturbances. In an extreme case of vitamin B_1 deficiency, a person becomes irritable, depressed, quarrelsome, uncooperative, fearful, and may even have disturbing dreams and ideas of persecution.

In a B-vitamin deficiency, a person may be depressed, emotionally unstable, irritable, confused, disoriented, perhaps even have hallucinations.

A person with a B_{12} deficiency may experience irritability, confusion, amnesia, and psychoses.

So what we know for sure is this: certain compounds, such as those found in dietary protein, are vital for brain function. Our brain is made up of a vast network of neurons that communicate with each other through the release of neurotransmitters. Certain vitamins and minerals are necessary in order for nerve impulses to be conducted. So in a very real sense, the food we eat feeds the brain.

You may be wondering, is a certain kind of diet better for the brain than another?

Research suggests this: a high-carbohydrate meal, let's say a high-sugar meal, lowers the blood levels of certain amino acids in the brain. *But* a high-protein meal increases those levels.

This tells us that too much sugar may inhibit certain brain functions. Some experiments have shown that people given a high protein meal showed more alertness and ability to concentrate than another group given a high carbohydrate meal. But eating too high a level of protein in the diet can have other adverse effects on the body. Balance is the key.

It is clear though, that food affects the working of our brain. But what about the soul? What about our spiritual lives?

Well, let's think about that. What we call our "conscience," the ability to tell right from wrong, is a function of reason. We need clear heads to make good moral decisions. That's the connection. Our thinking is affected by the brain tissues that are nourished from the food we eat.

There's also another connection—our will. There's a connection we can make between our will and adequate nutrition. Our reason might tell us what the right thing to do is. But we need a strong will to carry that out, to actually *do* the right thing. And we've seen that, especially, in cases of prolonged malnutrition, the will is affected; it is weakened.

Good nutrition affects our minds. Good nutrition affects our wills.

That's one important reason why caring for our bodies is part of caring for our souls. And that brings new meaning to something the apostle John wrote.

Look at his greeting in Third John: "Beloved, I pray that you may prosper in all things and be in health, just as your soul prospers" (3 John 2, NKJV).

Be in health—just as your soul prospers. Physical and spiritual health—they're tied together. The body and soul aren't enemies. They're part of a whole that God created.

Let's look at what the apostle Paul has to say on this subject. He's writing to the Thessalonians. And this is his prayer for them recorded here in 1 Thessalonians: "Now may the God of peace Himself sanctify you completely; and may your whole spirit, soul, and body be preserved blameless at the coming of our Lord Jesus Christ" (1 Thessalonians 5:23, NKJV).

The apostle longs for believers to be sanctified completely. That's what those desert hermits were trying to achieve—complete holiness. But Paul didn't recommend spiting the body to please the soul. He prayed that spirit, soul, and body would be preserved blameless.

Our physical health affects our minds. A clearer mind helps build a purer soul.

Here's the apostle Paul picturing true spirituality. He writes in Colossians: "If then you were raised with Christ, seek those things which are above, where Christ is, sitting at the right hand of God. Set your mind on things above, not on things on the earth" (Colossians 3:1, 2, NKJV).

Believers are urged—set your mind on things above. A key part of becoming spiritual is concentration. Focusing on Christ in heaven. Seeing Him at the right hand of God. Understanding that that world is as real as the world around us.

The author of Hebrews tells us that, in the race of life, we should "fix our eyes on Jesus, the author and perfecter of our faith" (Hebrews 12:2, NIV).

Keep looking at Jesus. That's important. And that requires a clear mind. Focusing on something you can't see right now requires concentration.

Yes, having a clear mind helps us nurture our souls. That's why it's so important not to put destructive things in our bodies. It's obvious that certain drugs play havoc on the body and mind.

But other substances affect us in more subtle ways. An addiction to caffeine can keep us from thinking clearly. People who keep gulping down coffee may be very wired up for a short period of time, but studies show that their judgment is going downhill.

A healthy body helps us think clearly. A healthy body also does something else: It gives us more energy. That's another reason caring for the body helps us nourish our souls. The fact is, caring for our souls requires energy; it requires strength.

Too often, we have a picture of the spiritual life as something very passive. Seeking God can seem a matter of just sitting and meditating. You don't do much. You become sort of a couch potato of the soul.

Well, what we don't realize is that even prayer and meditation require energy, inner strength. Those internal processes need to be energized in some way. That's why a purely passive lifestyle doesn't lend itself to spirituality very well. You tend to take the easiest course, follow the easiest impulses.

The book of Ecclesiastes offers this bit of wisdom: "eat at the proper time—for strength and not for drunkenness" (Ecclesiastes 10:17, NIV).

In other words, don't just eat to stuff yourself, to get so full that you feel woozy. Eat for strength. Eat what will nourish your body the best.

Caring for the soul requires energy, physical energy. So let me tell you a little about how to get more energy into your life.

The bottom line is something called exercise.

Exercise is an important key to wellness. It's one of the best ways of burning up excess fat. It improves circulation and helps normalize blood pressure. It provides more electrical current to the brain and nerve cells. It stimulates the immune system. And exercise actually stimulates the brain to produce a chemical that gives us a sense of well-being.

But most of all, exercise gives us energy. It may seem contradictory. It may seem that exercise just makes you tired. But in fact, a consistent program of exercise will make you feel much more energetic in the long run.

Doctors tell me a good rule of thumb is this. Engage in an exercise that is the equivalent of walking one mile in fifteen minutes—four or more times a week.

That's one mile at a brisk pace. Do that at least four times a week and you'll stay in good shape.

That's a way of taking care of your body. But it's also a way of taking care of your soul. Because our souls need energy too.

Now, let me tell you about the final reason that caring for our bodies helps us nurture our souls. This reason—our physical health glorifies God. A healthy body glorifies our Creator.

The apostle Paul once gave his fellow believers in Corinth this advice: "Therefore, whether you eat or drink, or whatever you do, do all to the glory of God" (1 Corinthians 10:31, NKJV).

Did you ever stop to think that our eating and drinking can be a way of praising God? How? These things glorify God if they keep the bodies He's given us in good health.

A healthy diet is a way of saying "Thank You" to our Creator, the Creator who fashioned our marvelous physical bodies. It's a way of showing Him respect.

In First Corinthians, Paul wrote: "the body is . . .

for the Lord, and the Lord for the body" (1 Corinthians 6:13, NKJV).

Our bodies are not just boxes that contain human souls. They have value. They are called temples of the Holy Spirit. Our health glorifies our Creator. Vibrant physical health is His plan for us no less than vibrant spiritual health.

One way we can glorify our Creator is to follow the diet that He prescribes. Maybe you never noticed, but we can glimpse how God planned to keep us in good health back at the beginning of the Bible, back in the Garden of Eden. We can examine the original diet given to Adam and Eve by their Creator.

Genesis contains part of God's very first instructions to human beings. After telling them to "be fruitful and multiply," He said: "I give you every seed-bearing plant on the face of the whole earth and every tree that has fruit with seed in it. They will be yours for food" (Genesis 1:29, NIV).

Every seed-bearing plant. And every tree that has fruit. In other words, the menu in the Garden of Eden contained this: selections from fruits, nuts, grains, and vegetables. The eating of meat did not begin until after sin entered the world.

I think this is quite remarkable. We now know that a low-fat, high-fiber diet of fruits and vegetables fights cancer and heart disease. The latest scientific research shows how these foods fight today's big killers.

And that is precisely the diet originally given to us by our Creator. Food, in its natural state, builds up the body's defenses.

I can tell you that a balanced vegetarian diet has had a positive impact on my life. My responsibilities as an evangelist create a lot of pressure. It involves a lot of time in airplanes, a lot of time in meetings, a lot of time presenting a message to large groups of people. It's quite a demanding schedule.

But I believe my vegetarian diet has been an important factor in my continued good health. So, I'm very glad the Seventh-day Adventist Church I belong to has emphasized this original diet and the importance of physical health in the Christian life. More and more people are now recognizing the Adventist contribution to public health.

So yes, eating healthy is a way to honor God, to glorify our Creator. It's a way of taking care of our souls.

Paul made a very eloquent appeal in his letter to believers in Rome. This is what he says: "I beseech you therefore, brethren, by the mercies of God, that you present your bodies a living sacrifice, holy, acceptable to God, which is your reasonable service" (Romans 12:1, NKJV).

Paul is making reference to Old Testament animal sacrifices. The spotless lamb laid on the altar and sacrificed to God was a way for people to express faith in the Messiah who would come and die for our sins.

But now, after Christ's death on the cross, Paul suggests we can make a better sacrifice. We can present living bodies to God, not dead ones. We can present our own bodies to Him, dedicated to Him. That's our reasonable service.

Healthy bodies are one way we can glorify God. And let me tell you something. You can be healthy even in a wheelchair. A quadriplegic can present his body to God as a living sacrifice. An invalid can present her body to Christ as a living sacrifice.

God doesn't demand perfect bodies from us. That's not the point at all. Some of us struggle with handicaps. Some of us struggle with chronic health problems. All God asks is that we give Him what we have. That's it. Lay it on the altar, He says, and I can make something beautiful out of it, something meaningful.

God just asks that we do our best to take care of what we've been given, that we live as healthy as we're able. For some people, taking a few steps in a rehab unit is all they can do. Well, those steps can be taken to the glory of God.

We can lay broken bodies on God's altar. We can lay whole bodies on the altar. In God's hands, both can become living sacrifices that display His glory.

Yes, caring for our bodies can help us think more clearly; it can give us more energy; it can glorify God.